Everyday Writing

Everyday Writing

*Tips and prompts to fit your
regularly scheduled life*

Midge Raymond

www.AshlandCreekPress.com

Everyday Writing

Tips and prompts to fit your regularly scheduled life

Published by Ashland Creek Press
www.ashlandcreekpress.com

ISBN 978-1-61822-011-0
Library of Congress Control Number: 2012930037

Printed in the United States of America on acid-free paper.
All paper products used to create this book are Sustainable
Forestry Initiative (SFI) Certified Sourcing.

"...seek [that] which your own everyday life offers you; describe your sorrows and desires, passing thoughts and the belief in some sort of beauty—describe all these with loving, quiet, humble sincerity, and use, to express yourself, the things in your environment, the images from your dreams, the objects of your memory."
—Rainer Maria Rilke, *Letters to a Young Poet*

Contents

When life gets in the way of your writing...

I wrote this book for people like me. For those who have a passion for writing but never quite enough time. For writers who want to make progress on their stories and novels while continuing to make ends meet. For people who want to live the writer's life but can only spare a few minutes a day.

You don't need to quit your day job in order to be a writer; you don't need to put off having children or wait until retirement to start your novel. You need to become an Everyday Writer, which means seeing the world as a writer does even when you may not have the time to get the words on the page.

Whether you're a writer with a day job, a stay-at-home-parent, or a freelancer, finding time for creative work is always a challenge. The paid work comes first, not to mention the family, the bills, the pets, the home repairs, and everything else that needs doing. And then, when you finally do carve out time to write, suddenly even the most tedious of chores can seem so much more inviting than the blank page. (At least, this is what happens to me.)

It feels like sacrilege to say that I don't write every single day, but it's true. And that doesn't mean I'm not still a writer; as you'll see in the following chapters, being a writer involves far more than sitting down somewhere and typing.

While I'm the first to agree that a daily writing practice can be invaluable, I don't subscribe to the notion that if we don't sit down to write every day, we'll never accomplish anything—and yet writers are often told just that, in various ways. Being an Everyday Writer is not about putting daily words on a page but about seeing the world as a writer and recognizing the myriad ways in which your everyday life informs your work. And this, in turn, *will* put words on the page.

Let's face it—we can't all be full-time creative writers, with quiet rooms of our own overlooking the ocean or the mountains. But we *can* find room to write in our everyday lives, from paying more attention to our surroundings to carving out writing weekends to going on an annual retreat. We need to find different ways to create both mental and physical space for our work.

What is everyday writing?

Every writer has his or her own ideal routine; you simply need to discover yours. You don't need to give up the day job to be a writer—in fact, I highly recommend embracing it. For one, there's a lot of fantastic material there; two, it provides a sense of structure that many of us feel a little lost without. I find that the more time I have, the more time I waste, so being busy actually helps motivate me to fit in writing time. Over the years, I've known many writers, myself included, who have left their jobs to write, only to watch the year (or years) go by without writing much at all.

Meanwhile, we can keep in mind that even the most famous and successful writers started out with day jobs, squeezing in their writing whenever and wherever they could. Toni Morrison worked in publishing. Stephen King worked in a laundry and taught English. Raymond Carver was a farm worker, delivery boy, and night janitor. William Carlos Williams was a pediatrician. Scott Turow was (and still is) an attorney.

Everyday writing is about getting it done, no matter how it happens and no matter how long it takes. If you're motivated, you can and will fit in your writing. The when and where isn't what's important. What matters is that you think like a writer—which in turn makes it impossible not to write.

So you'll need to create a schedule that works for you, whether it's getting up two hours before the kids, stopping at the library for an hour after work, or spending weekend mornings on your writing. It doesn't have to be every single day, and, like an exercise regimen, it can be good to do something a little different each time. But do build some writing time into your life until it becomes a habit that feels both necessary and good. And, more important, you'll need to adopt the identity of Writer, which this book aims to help you achieve—and again, once you're there, you'll find that you're unable *not* to make the time to write.

In all my years of teaching, one of the questions that comes up most often is what to do about writer's block. The scenario: You've set aside time to write; you've got one hour until the kids get up; you're sitting there, and absolutely nothing is happening. This is where the prompts come in.

How to be an everyday writer (without writing every day)

This book is divided into two parts. The first offers tips for helping you step into the role of Writer and to maintain that identity from here forward, no matter what other hats you may also wear in your life. The second offers more than 150 writing exercises, from five-minute prompts you can do on your busiest days to longer prompts you can do on a writing retreat—and everything in between.

The prompts in this book are for all writers, whether you're a novelist, memoirist, or poet, and they can be written from your own personal experience, from the point of view of one of your fictional characters, or even from the POV of a real character from your own life (a family member, a friend, a pet, etc.). For the most part, I use the *you* voice here, but always feel free to take an exercise in any direction you'd like—there are absolutely no rules. The longer prompts tend to be more generative in nature, but they are all geared toward jump-starting your work, whether by prompting new memories, developing a new character, or resolving an issue in a scene or story.

Keep in mind that you can come back to these prompts again and again—if you get bogged down in a story, take a prompt and apply it to a key character in that scene; if you need a break from your novel, try one of these prompts as an exercise in personal writing. Writing exercises can help our writing in ways we don't know until we do them. They can, for instance, allow our minds to retreat from the puzzle of a current project and wander a bit, perhaps leading us back to the puzzle from a different angle and getting us closer to a solution. Writing prompts can help us discover new material for an old piece, or new material for a new piece—or they can help inform whatever it is we're working on. Or, sometimes best of all, they can take us places we never knew existed, and lead us right into the next poem or story or novel.

Once, in response to one of my e-newsletter's writing prompts (*Describe what's on your bedside table. And why.*), a writer told me she didn't actually do the exercise, but she did clean up her bedside table. I loved that—it's progress of a different sort, but who's to say that having a clean bedside table can't lead to clearer thoughts and better dreams? And, perhaps by extension, more vivid writing.

Life and Writing need not be mutually exclusive— at least not all the time. Almost everything you do, and every place you go, can lead to a story idea or a poem. The prompts in this book will offer you exercises to build upon, whether you're in your writing space looking for inspiration or in line at the post office looking for distraction. This book is designed to help you develop these skills—the skills of an everyday writer—in which you'll see the world in a way less ordinary, and you'll be creating far more, and more often, than you imagined.

Part 1:
Becoming an everyday writer

Tips for creating a writing life

Whether you're just beginning or have been writing for years, it's always helpful to think about your life, your writing space, your routines—and to assess how well they're working for you.

If all is going well and you feel like a happy, productive writer, you're all set.

If not, take this opportunity to shake things up.

I'm always in the process of shaking things up. Thanks to a busy work schedule, I still don't have a set time of day to write, even when I'm in the middle of a project. In a way, this is a good thing: When I'm really into something, I never want to limit my writing to some predetermined amount of time. But when I'm in a more challenging phase—say, that horrible first-draft stage—I have to work harder to stay inspired.

So what I do to keep a project going is set goals

rather than dates and times. This way, I can be flexible about when and where I write but still get the work done. Some days, I'm able to devote four hours to writing; other days, I'm lucky to write for half an hour. When I find myself blocked, I'll do writing prompts or even a little research, which may not result in words on the page but nevertheless keeps the project moving forward. If I find that I simply can't stare at the computer any longer, I'll take a notebook somewhere—and the change in perspective is almost always illuminating.

Here are a few tips for creating—and maintaining—your own writing life.

Outline your goals.

As someone who has to grab snippets of time where she can, I find it helpful to look at my goals in terms of long-term, short-term, and immediate. If, for example, you want to write a novel, that's definitely a long-term goal—so how will you break it up into manageable pieces? This is where short-term and immediate goals come in—and unless you've been doing this for a while and know your writing self well, you may have to experiment. So, for example, you might create a short-term goal of writing a chapter a month, and an immediate goal of writing

500 words a day, three days a week. Figure out what works best with your schedule, and take baby steps toward your larger goal. Always remain open to revising your schedule, which will allow you to keep going rather than get overwhelmed and give up.

Know that you can write anywhere.

I wrote my first published short story in a tiny corner of a railroad flat in New York City. When I moved to an even smaller apartment after that (which I didn't think was possible), I wrote at university libraries. Recently I've been writing in a sun-drenched studio with a marvelous view. And you know what? The space doesn't matter one bit; the struggles are the same, and the work either gets done or it doesn't. All you need to do is find a corner of the world to call your writing space. Even if you don't have enough room at home (and you'd be surprised by how little you need), you can find it somewhere.

Be observant.

As a fiction writer with a journalism background, I've always thought of myself as a keen observer. (Don't we all?) Then one evening my illusion was shattered. I was sitting with several people in a park near a duck pond. We were all watching the ducks, as well as the two little kids standing near the edge—then we looked up to see three young men passing by. The men were walking off the designated path, which is probably what got our attention—and moments later, my husband said, "I wonder what he was doing with that gun?"

And I said, "What gun?"

My husband, who will insist we're out of peanut butter while staring into a pantry with three jars of it right in front of him, was very pleased to have caught something I'd missed (this rarely happens). And for once, his eyes weren't deceiving him; someone else had seen exactly what he had: One of the young men who'd passed by was carrying a large handgun on a holster, right out in the open.

And all I remembered was that one of the guys wore a green T-shirt.

Realizing I'm not nearly as observant as I think I am was a huge wake-up call, and it has inspired me to keep my eyes and ears open just a bit more than I think I need to. I still probably miss quite a lot, though I hope not nearly as much as I missed that day in the park. Always remind yourself that some of the best material—whether for a new story idea or a finely wrought description—comes to us when we're paying attention.

Make your writing space a special one.

Wherever your writing space is, make it a place you want to be—and one you want to keep returning to. If you're writing in the tiniest corner of your kitchen table, for example, you might surround yourself with books to block the view of the blender. If you're in a cubby at the library, bring headphones to tune out noise, or leave the laptop at home and write by hand, which can be very freeing. Do what you can in order to view your writing time as a treat rather than a chore.

Set your own rules and ask others to respect them.

I still remember the first time I phoned my friend Judy Reeves and got her voice mail, which told me, "If you're calling before 1:00 p.m., this is my writing time. I'll get back to you after 1:00." This was a revelation to me at the time, and I've since done my best to follow her wonderful example. Ask the people in your life to take your writing time as seriously as you do. Remember that you don't have to be published to be a legitimate writer; you don't have to explain or prove yourself in any way. Just ask that your writing time is respected, and be firm about it.

Be flexible.

Whether you've set aside time in the early hours of the morning or the late hours of the night, eventually you're likely to be struck with some form of writer's block. You can use this time to get some extra sleep (the subconscious can do wonders), or simply to do something else that's related, even tangentially, to your work. Research. Read. Watch a film set in the era in which your novel takes place. Listen to the type of music your character listens to. Even these little things can help create a mood that will inspire you and help get you back into the work (see the section **How to write when you're not really writing** for more on this).

Be patient.

Be ready to take the long view toward your work. While we'd all love to have our writing flow smoothly into perfectly polished drafts—not to mention to have a project snapped up by the first editor who reads it—this rarely happens. The process of producing good writing is laborious (and sometimes tedious), and there are no shortcuts. Embrace the fact that you're not likely to churn out a perfect story or poem on the first try—and you'll enjoy it that much more simply by not fighting it. This doesn't mean giving yourself permission to procrastinate or to leave work unfinished; it simply means respecting the process. Same goes for publication, which also takes time; see below.

Be persistent.

From Margaret Mitchell (whose best-selling, Pulitzer Prize–winning *Gone with the Wind* was rejected by more than three dozen publishers) to J. K. Rowling (who went through a year of submissions and a dozen rejections before Harry Potter eventually made her the world's first billionaire writer), published authors know that success doesn't come easily or quickly. If you're trying to get a short story published, you'll discover that the top-tier literary magazines publish less than 1 percent of the submissions they receive. It's tough out there, and dedication and persistence may be among the most important traits a writer can have. Try to embrace rejection, and even celebrate it, as a necessary (and temporary) obstacle on the road to becoming a published author. I've had stories accepted after more than fifty rejections (yes, fifty—that wasn't a typo), and I had one story rejected by more than forty magazines before it was accepted, published, and nominated for a Pushcart Prize. The lesson is, always, don't give up. Ever. (See **Accepting rejection** for more on this lovely topic.)

Carry a notebook.

You probably already do—but if not, start now. My favorite ideas have come to me in random places, and if I hadn't written them down, they'd have been lost forever. And carrying a notebook is also a great reminder that no matter where you are, you're a writer.

Clear writing space = clear mind

Your writing space, wherever it may be, should be clean, neat, inviting—a place you want to return to again and again. Sometimes showing up is half the battle: We're motivated by what's appealing, much the way we're more enthusiastic about exercising on a gorgeous, sunny day than a gloomy, rainy one. If your writing space is appealing, you'll want to show up there all the more.

So wherever your writing space may be, create it exactly as you want it—but do beware of clutter. You may need a lot of books on hand, but avoid piling them up next to the computer. You may have taken a lot of notes as part of your research, but don't let them gather and scatter all over the desk. And whatever you do, don't stack the bills, the mail, or anything else not related to your writing in this space. (If you must, invest in a file folder or cabinet so that these things can at least be out of sight while you're writing.)

If your space needs a little work, take half an hour of your next dedicated writing session to do a little spring cleaning. Get rid of everything except what you need in order to write. You'll be amazed: Clearing the desk truly does clear the mind.

Of course, we can't always have this level of order in our lives, so flexibility is key; clutter will likely find its way back into your writing space eventually. So, as a rule, try to spend a little time each month revising your workspace so that it fits your writing needs.

You might also try some sort of meditation before you enter the writing zone. Do whatever works for you, whether it's a twenty-minute session in the lotus position or simply straightening your spine and taking three long, deep breaths. Just allow yourself a few moments to leave one world behind as you prepare to enter another.

My name is [insert name], and I'm a [insert social network]-aholic...

In case you're wondering whether you do, in fact, have a social media addiction, here's a little quiz for you:

- Do you check your smartphone for email, voicemail, Facebook updates, etc., before you get out of bed?

- Do you email, play games, text, tweet, etc., when in line at the post office/bank/wherever?

- Have you ever texted while at a meal with a loved one?

- Do you often feel overwhelmed, time-strapped, snarky?

- When you sit down to write, do you feel... A) inspired and focused; B) scattered and stressed?

If you've answered "yes" to any of the first four and/ or chose "B" for the last one, you've probably got a bit of a problem. (For the record, so do I.) But there is hope for us. All we need to do is unplug a little bit.

For most of us—and particularly for us writers— there's a fine line between being connected and being addicted. We want and need to connect to our community of writers, whether it's to promote a book or to seek advice—but the downside is that this time online is time taken away from our writing.

I remember an evening in Seattle's Pike Place Market (which offers some of the best people-watching ever) when I arrived early to meet a friend for happy hour. As I waited for my friend and our table, I pulled out my phone—just to check email. Then to check Facebook. Then to play a couple rounds of Words with Friends. Then to text my husband.

What I realized later, as I chatted with my friend, a poet, about writing and publishing and technology, was how much I'd missed out on by having my nose buried in my phone. I'd barely registered the couple waiting next to me, growing more impatient by the moment, exchanging irritable whispers in that way couples do so it won't seem as if they're actually arguing in public. I'd hardly glanced at the tourists wandering in, the group celebrating someone's birthday. While normally I'd have been eavesdropping and otherwise taking mental notes, I'd pretty much ignored it all.

The gadgets we have offer great ways to pass the time, but since that evening I've been making an effort to remember the old days, when I had to look outward to pass the time—when I used to watch and listen. And, more often than not, I ended up with great story ideas or snippets of dialogue.

It goes without saying that the more "connected" we are, technically speaking, the more disconnected we become from the real world—and for writers, this isn't a good thing. Turning to the virtual world takes us away from the solitary pleasures writers should enjoy: all those interesting people to observe, all those fascinating conversations to overhear. So, unless I have a pressing email to return, I've vowed to ignore that enticing little screen when I'm in line at the post office and to look around me instead.

If you, too, have an online addiction problem, below are a few tips.

Take at least one day a week off the Internet.

Okay, if that's a little too ambitious, try one day a

month. Make it a holiday, a weekend day—a quiet time when you won't feel as though you'll miss out on much. It's a start, and I think you'll find that the more you're able to detach, the more you'll enjoy it.

Turn off your phone when you write.

If you have kids with a sitter or otherwise need to be available for emergencies, pretend you're at the opera: Leave it on vibrate, and answer only if necessary.

Disconnect from the Internet during your writing time.

Stay entirely offline during your writing sessions, even if you literally have to unplug your Internet connection to accomplish this. If you're tempted to hop online briefly, to check an online dictionary or do some research, resist. (We all know how easily those five minutes online can turn into an hour or more.) Instead, jot down what you need to look up and give yourself a few minutes at the end of your writing session to take care of it. Seek out a café that doesn't offer Internet access, and go there. And stay there.

Turn your phone off before bed.

Better yet, disconnect a couple hours before bedtime, if possible. This will relax your mind in ways that can open up your creativity. (If you use your phone as an alarm clock, put it in "airplane mode" so that it'll wake you up but still allow you to be free of phone calls and text messages.)

How to write when you're not really writing...

Sometimes it's a kid coming down with the flu. Or a project at work requiring serious overtime. Or the sun shining for the first time in forty-seven days, and you absolutely must get your Vitamin D the natural way. Whatever it is, sometimes we just aren't able—or willing—to sit down and write.

But just because you're not sitting at the computer doesn't mean you can't be working. There are a lot of ways to "write"—even when you're not actually writing. Here are a few ideas.

Do your research.

Research is vital to any writing you do—the more accurate, detailed, and vivid your characters, stories, and language, the more alive your work will feel to the reader. In nonfiction, accuracy is essential for obvious reasons—in fiction, it's essential for less obvious but equally important reasons: If your readers are getting stuck on the credibility of your plot or your depiction of a certain locale, this means you're losing them.

And you can do a great deal of research simply by paying attention, carrying your notebook, and writing things down. You can also enter into conversations with people who cross your path in the community whose lives or work may be different from your own, whether it's the local arborist, a computer programmer, or a vegan chef. Keep your eyes and ears open, and don't be shy. See the section **It's okay to be nosy (sometimes)** for more on research.

Read a book.

If you find yourself in for a long wait at the pediatrician's office or booking a flight for a last-minute business trip, bring along your research. Whether a novel or a biography, reading something related to your project will help you stay in the writing zone. And if you're reading a novel, ask yourself how you might have improved upon the book if you were the author. Better yet, rewrite a scene or two. And make a habit of bookmarking sentences and phrases that stick with you. Study what it is you like about them, and use this to improve your own work.

See a film.

If you're going stir crazy in the world of words, immerse yourself in the world of images. It gives the brain a wonderful break to focus on something different for a while, and this can actually open the mind to solving problems in your writing. In fact, most writers I know have their biggest epiphanies when they are not actually writing but brushing their teeth, taking a walk, driving to work—all sorts of everyday things can offer moments of reflection and revelation. A film does, of course, require attention—but it also allows you to sit back and relax a bit. So go to the movies. Whether you're writing about war, cooking, or relationships, opt for something that will enlighten or inform your work.

Listen to music.

Music is an excellent way to get into the setting of your novel or the mood of your poem. If your novel is set in the 1980s, listen to music from this period during your commute. If you get writer's block, take a walk with a playlist that your character might listen to. And don't neglect music while you're writing: If you're among the many writers who can't handle lyrics while they write, try classical music, or an opera in a foreign language—anything that aligns with the mood of whatever you're working on or that can provide a soundtrack for your work that further enhances the story.

Pay attention during the boring moments.

No matter where you are (sitting in traffic, squeezed onto the bus, waiting for someone at a restaurant), look around you. Listen to conversations; study people's faces. Get into the habit of doing this, and you'll notice how much it sharpens your eye for detail and your ear for dialogue. And (of course) be sure you have your notebook handy. The vast majority of my stories begin like this: by overhearing a line of dialogue or seeing something out of the corner of my eye. In *Forgetting English*, the inspiration for my story "Rest of World" came from seeing a couple praying at a Japanese temple; I was inspired to write "Never Turn Your Back on the Ocean" as I watched a nanny usher her charges into an elevator at a Hawaiian resort. Whenever I hear or see something interesting, I jot it down and let my imagination take over—and this is how stories happen.

Watch (good) television.

On those nights—or holiday weekends—when you

feel too tired or brain-dead to write, go ahead and channel surf. But again, choose carefully: Look for a program that relates to your current project. Not only might you learn something new, it'll give you renewed zeal for the work, and you might realize you've got a few words in you after all.

A brief note...

Keep in mind that these tips are not substitutes for writing, nor are they excuses for not writing. They're just ways to stay in the game when you're otherwise unable to get in your daily word count. To avoid losing momentum, you probably won't want to take more than a couple days away from a project (until you're done, that is; that's when it needs the breathing room), but you can use these tips to remain attached to your work, even when you're not actively writing.

It's okay to be nosy (sometimes)

A couple of years ago, I created a medical center in Seattle. I'm not a billionaire philanthropist (unfortunately)—rather, I am a fiction writer who, in the middle of a scene, realized I needed to put one of my characters in a trauma center. And while there are myriad hospitals to choose from in Seattle, I discovered that it would be a whole lot easier to make one up.

With a background in journalism, I'm a stickler for accuracy—and this trait has followed me into fiction. However, I've also learned when it's important and necessary to spend time on research—and when it's not. You don't want to spend hours researching what will end up being a couple of throwaway lines in a chapter, but you do want to put the time in when you need information for credibility or for historical or emotional accuracy.

For example: Anytime I'm depicting a real place, I study it—I'll visit it myself if I can; if I'm not able to, I look at photos, research its history, and talk to people who have visited and/or lived there. On the other hand, my Seattle medical center came about when I found myself spending far too much time researching Seattle's hospitals, trying to figure out where my fictional patient would likely have been taken given her location and the nature of her trauma—then I realized that I could spend all day on that, and it wouldn't be worth it. What was important in the scene at hand wasn't the hospital itself but what happened to the character. So I let my journalistic self off the hook, made up a fake hospital, and moved on to what I needed to write.

Being an everyday writer means fitting in your work whenever you can—and research will often be a vital part of your writing. So even when you're unable to sit down to write, always be aware of the research you can be doing, whether you've got a few extra minutes for a web search on your phone or you meet someone who might be able to help you sharpen the details of a character's job. Below are a few tips for making the most of your time to research.

Get up close and personal.

While the Internet is an invaluable research tool, the info you're getting may not always be accurate, and you can't always verify the credibility of your sources. So often the best way to get information is to get it firsthand. Go to where you need to be. I'd never have been able to write with authority about a medium-security men's prison until I spent an afternoon in one; even though I've read many books about the 1989 student uprisings in Tiananmen Square, it wasn't until I interviewed one of the leaders of the movement that I truly felt the passion the students had for their cause and understood what they'd sacrificed. Make an effort to spend time with the people you need to in order to do the best research—and try to spend this time in their natural habitats, where you'll be able to become intimately aware of what they do and what's at stake.

You may be wondering, "How do I get access to these people and places?" But before you despair, realize that you have more at your fingertips than you know. Think about your family and friends, your writers' group, your colleagues, your neighbors: Among their talents and professions, you will most likely find that one of them has the information you need, or knows someone who does. Whether you want firsthand information on how to prepare a witness for trial or want to know what it's like to work the night shift in a psychiatric hospital, if you ask around, chances are you'll find someone who can point you in the right direction. And even if you can't find a connection, don't hesitate to reach out to professionals on your own. While I might first rely on my network of friends and family, I've also had to make my share of cold calls, from police officers to neurologists, and I've nearly always gotten warm and helpful responses. So pick up the phone or send out an e-mail. Explain your project and see what happens. You will never know unless you ask—and you'll probably find, as I have, that people are amazingly generous and that they love to share their knowledge and talk about what they do.

Be (a little) nosy.

If you're doing an interview for the purpose of research, ask any question you can think of. If you think it might be too personal, tread softly and assure your subject that he or she need not answer it—but do ask it. Nine times out of ten you'll get an answer.

Even in everyday conversation, if you find yourself talking to someone whose insight might be helpful, ask questions that might inform your project. You should always be up-front about being a writer when you talk to someone about what they do—but often it'll happen in the opposite order: You'll have an interesting conversation and realize later that it has sparked a story idea. Either way, being a little nosy is a good thing (though you do want to avoid being overly so lest you find that no one will talk to you at all).

Take a ridiculous amount of notes.

When you interview people, while they generally expect note-taking, it still may seem odd to them at first; however, they'll eventually ignore the fact that you're scribbling away. (If you use a recorder, always take notes as well; electronic devices can never be counted on.) Write down every single thing you can, even if it doesn't seem significant in the moment; you'll always want to have far more information than you can use because you never know what might become relevant later.

Take photos.

You may look touristy, but places fade from our memories faster than we think. And if you're gathering information about a specific place, no matter how much you've written down, having visual notes will come in handy later. When it comes to taking photos of people, be aware and respectful of any privacy

issues or of making the subjects uncomfortable—
good research is wonderful; restraining orders aren't
so much.

Talk to people, and listen to them.

Every region has a local dialect of some sort; every
place has nicknames for landmarks, shops, taverns,
etc. Find out what they are so that you can feel
assured that any local will approve of your depiction
of a certain setting. Likewise, every career has its
own unique jargon; learn it so that you can write
with authority. And every character has a unique
way of speaking—by listening to others and noting
different words, language tics, and speaking styles,
you'll avoid the common dialogue problem of every
character sounding just like you.

How to meet your writing goals

At some point in time (usually when a new year rolls around), we'll look at our writing goals and realize we haven't accomplished everything we'd hoped to. Yet that doesn't mean we can't re-evaluate and move on; the worst thing to do is to get discouraged and give up. In fact, taking stock of what we've accomplished (or not) can be inspiring—especially if you check in with yourself and your writing goals midyear rather than at the very end.

The first thing you'll want to do is outline your goals (see page 12). Once you've aligned what you can realistically accomplish with your regularly scheduled life, you're ready for the next challenge: actually meeting these goals.

Be organized.

I keep running lists of works I've published, works in progress, and works I'm submitting—and this pretty much covers everything. Every writer organizes work differently; whether you use an Excel spreadsheet or a loose-leaf binder, find a way to track what you're working on and keep it up-to-date. Each list serves myriad purposes: Your list of publications, for example, will help you determine whether you might have enough stories or poems for a collection; even better, it's written proof of all that you've accomplished so far. A list of works in progress will ensure that you don't inadvertently lose track of a great idea and will remind you of what you need to do to meet your goals. A submissions list will keep you from making embarrassing mistakes like submitting the same piece twice to any one publication; it'll also be invaluable to visit when you have new work that's ready to submit (keep detailed notes on responses, too—for example, if you get a good rejection, this publication should be at the top of your list when you're ready to submit a new piece).

Check in and track your progress.

Taking inventory will help you see what you've begun and how far you've come—and how far you still need to go. This isn't meant to stress you out about what you're not writing but to inspire you to stay on course. You may find that you haven't gotten anywhere with the novel you'd hoped to write but that you found the perfect ending for a short story you've been working on for years. Or you may find that the poem you started isn't coming together but that it would make a better personal essay anyway. Looking at your works in progress every month will help you stay on track; try a calendar reminder to make sure you do it. If monthly check-ins don't fit in with your schedule, try every two months, or every three. At the very minimum, I recommend setting goals every January, re-evaluating every June, and re-assessing every December.

Don't dismiss unfinished projects.

I've found many gems in long-abandoned projects. One reason is that I write everything down; even when I have only a vague idea for a story, I'll jot down a few notes, file it as a "story in progress," and come back to it at least once a year. Often it just sits there for another year, but sometimes I'll find it at just the right time, and it'll come to life in new and surprising ways. Never abandon old ideas; you never know when they'll suddenly be relevant. Revisit all your "old" stories, poems, or essays at least once a year.

Be open to recycling.

Always look for ways in which to get your work in front of as many readers as possible. While most publications don't accept previously published work, look for ones that do and see if you have anything appropriate. Look for awards to submit to. See how you can use new work to better promote the work that's already out there. As an example, when *Forgetting English* was reissued in an expanded version with two new stories, I set out to find a home for a story that hadn't yet been published on its own—and when this story, "Lost Art," appeared online, its publication helped promote the collection as a whole. You might also do guest blogs or magazine articles; there are many ways to "build your platform," as they say in publishing—and if publishing a book is your ultimate goal, you'll want to fit in these little things that can go a long way in the end.

Accepting rejection

Rejection is never fun—yet it's a necessary, albeit unpleasant, part of every writer's life. I once read that the average short story is rejected twenty-five times before finding a home—and I've had stories accepted after twice as many rejections. And if I hadn't grown a thick skin and kept sending my stories out, they'd still be unpublished. So accepting rejection can help immeasurably in terms of staying the course, i.e., getting the work done and continuing to send it out. Below are a few suggestions for coping with rejection and keeping yourself and your writing going.

Be stubborn.

As I always tell my students, I am by no means any more talented than anyone else; if I get published more often than the next writer, it's simply because I'm a little more stubborn. If I've written a story I like, I'll send it out until it gets accepted, no matter how many rejections it takes. Over my years of teaching, I've seen talented writers give up after just one or two rejections, not understanding that it's not personal, that it's just part of the process. And I've seen diligent writers achieve great success simply by putting themselves and their work out there, over and over again. So keep this in mind and know that whatever happens, you have to keep writing and submitting.

Save your rejections.

When I first started submitting short stories, many years ago, I'd toss my rejection slips into a file folder (yes, this was so long ago that electronic submissions did not yet exist). Eventually I had to trade this file folder for an accordion folder just to hold them all, and this eventually got so overstuffed that I exchanged it for a large box that I kept in the basement. It wasn't until years later, when I had to move, that I went through all the rejections—and I was so glad I'd kept them. Reviewing these rejections was a tangible reminder of how far I'd come over the years, and I think every writer should be reminded of this once in a while.

I know writers who put rejections on the fridge along with their kids' artwork, as well as writers who celebrate good rejections as if they've gotten an acceptance—as they should. If you get a personal response of any kind (i.e., the editor uses your name instead of "Dear Author" or he/she says something specific about your story), then this is the sort of rejection you should, in fact, celebrate (see below).

Celebrate your rejections.

We tend to forget that being rejected is actually a great sign: It means you've finished something and sent it out; it means your work has been read by someone who takes you seriously as a writer. And this— especially if you've received a personal note from a busy editor—is worth celebrating.

You can also celebrate the normal rejections—have fun and be a little creative about it. As an example, at the literary organization San Diego Writers, we once held a literary salon in which about twenty writers gathered, shared rejection stories, and ceremoniously shredded our most egregious rejection slips (we wanted a bonfire, but the local fire code wouldn't allow for it). We also voted on the best and worse rejection letters and gave prizes for each. It was a fabulous evening of catharsis, unity, and inspiration. You're not alone in receiving that dreaded email or quarter-page slip of paper, so reach out and commiserate.

It's not you, it's me
(how and when to revise)

There comes a time in every project when one of two things will happen: It's working out very well, and you're ready to do a final revision—or something is wrong, and you're not sure what to do.

Let's tackle that one first. Sometimes a project just isn't working out—not the way you'd like it to, anyway. You'll find yourself worrying about it, thinking such thoughts as *I'm sorry, but it's just not working out between us* and *I need some time to think things over* and *Perhaps we should spend a little time apart*. And, finally: *It's not you, it's me*.

Being immersed in a writing project is not unlike a relationship: It's exciting at first (*I love my novel*), then the reality sets in (*This is going to be a lot of work*), and then perhaps it doesn't end up as you hoped (*Maybe this isn't such a good fit after all*). If this is the case, here are a few ways to help you decide whether your project is meant to be, or whether it was just a short-term, casual thing.

Get by with a little help from your (writing) friends.

Reach out to fellow writers to see if they've dealt with similar issues; most likely they have, and they can prescribe time, patience, alcohol, or whatever. It just helps to know that, like a relationship, a writing project sometimes gets off to a bad start, hits a rough patch, or needs a serious intervention. All of this is okay; it's part of the process. And sometimes we need an outside opinion as to what the problem might be.

Get some feedback.

Ask your mentor, writing partner, or writing group for a brainstorming session. Sometimes writers need to take a big step back from their pages and look at a project as a whole: where it's been, where it is now, where it's headed, and how it's going to get there.

Weigh your options.

Picture yourself giving up on your project completely.

Whether it's a story, a poem, or a novel, is this something that you can give up forever? Or set aside and come back to later? Or is it a story you must tell now? If the idea of setting it aside fills you with relief, then this is a clear sign. If you can't imagine giving up on it, then continue (though maybe not right away; see below).

Spend a little time apart.

As much as you may love and adore your writing project, all that togetherness isn't necessarily a good thing. Just as a relationship can get stifling when a couple spends every moment together, so a story needs to breathe on its own a bit. By taking some time away from whatever you're working on, you might gain a new perspective on it, appreciate new and different things about it, and/or bring something fresher to the keyboard or notebook next time you show up. You can always work on something else in the meantime—and you never know when you may be seeing each other regularly again, and maybe even heading toward happily ever after.

Know that recycling is an option.

If you do come to the conclusion that your project

isn't going to work out, hang on to everything you've accomplished so far. Even if the project isn't right for you at this time in your life (and timing is everything), you'll want to have kept all those gems you came up with during the process to use for another project. And know that it was worthwhile: If it doesn't work out in the end, your time and energy with that project will nonetheless have made you a better writer.

☽

If, on the other hand, your project has gone well and you're ready for the next phase—revision—I would still recommend spending a little time apart. You may need a month away; you may need only a week—it depends on how long you've been working on the project and how well you're able to distance yourself from it. But the first and most important part of good revision is to step back and return to it as fresh as possible, with an objective and critical eye, so that you're able to acknowledge its good points as well as its weak spots. Once you've done that, here are a few additional guidelines...

Look at the big picture first.

Assess story, structure, pacing, theme, setting, dialogue, and character before tackling your work scene-by-scene and word for word—and especially before worrying about comma splices. Once the overall story is flowing, then you can sweat the small stuff.

Do something drastic.

If something's not flowing, don't be afraid to make huge changes, such as putting the beginning at the end, or starting the story in media res; this is the time to experiment, and you've got nothing to lose. Just be sure to save each draft as you go, in case you decide to go back to an original version.

Don't be afraid to trim.

It may be hard to cut sentences or paragraphs you love, but be ruthless and see what happens. You might discover wonderful results—and if you don't, you can always revert to your original. But you won't know unless you try.

Consult a trusted reader.

Enlist a fellow writer or a professional editor to help you identify what needs the most work. Be sure to find someone who will be honest with you and offer you constructive feedback.

Try this checklist.

Below is a checklist I use whenever I finish a piece— or, more accurately, when I *think* I've finished a piece. Often I think I'm done until I go through this list, at which point I usually realize I still have quite a bit of work to do. But I keep this checklist handy and have found it very helpful in identifying what I need to work on.

- Does the piece hold together structurally?

- Is every scene necessary?

- Is there enough context/background?

- Are the ideas coming across clearly?

- Is the tone/POV consistent?

- Is the vocabulary well chosen?

- Would I find this piece engaging as a reader?

- Does the title work?

- Am I proud of it?

Create your own writing retreat

Writing retreats and residencies provide necessary havens for busy writers. Such opportunities are provided by organizations and institutions, with writers either earning scholarships or paying fees, and offer space ranging from one week to up to six months, in accommodations that vary from rustic to luxurious. The one thing they all provide is a room in which to write without distraction.

Retreats aren't for everyone, however—perhaps you don't have enough time off, or you don't yet have a writing sample for a retreat application; maybe you aren't able to travel very far. But there's no reason you can't create your own writing retreat at any time, for any length of time, whenever you need to. And even a few hours of retreat time is better than none at all.

So how to begin? Depending on your circumstances and on how you do your best writing, you can get together with fellow writers for a DIY retreat, or you can plan a "virtual" retreat.

If you like togetherness, compile a list of friends who are as strapped for writing time as you are and contact them to see about the possibilities. Does anyone have a vacation home that you can use for free? How many of you are available for a long weekend at the same time? Can someone simply donate her living room for an entire Saturday for a mini-retreat?

If you're a solo writer, another option is to create a virtual writing retreat. All you need to do is pick a day, weekend, or even a whole week, and commit to writing during that time—say, for an entire Sunday in March, or for three hours every weekday afternoon. But don't keep your plan to yourself: By getting other writers on board, you'll feel both inspired and accountable. Ask fellow writers to join you virtually and to commit to a common goal; this way, you'll feel as though you're part of an event even as you do your work in solitude.

Here are a few tips for making your retreat as efficient, enjoyable, and productive as possible.

Just do it.

My first virtual writing retreat was completely last-minute and completely unplanned. I wasn't even thinking about doing such a thing until I found myself, while writing an email to a friend, realizing that I absolutely had to get some writing done. So I decided, mid-email, that I was going to spend the entire weekend writing, and I told my friend about it. The next thing I knew, my friend had decided to do the same, announced it on Facebook, and invited a few other writing friends to join us virtually. All of a sudden, we had a community of writers, and it was enough of a public event that I couldn't flake out or make excuses—I was committed. You don't need to do a lot of planning; just make it happen.

Gather your fellow writers together.

Whether virtually or in person, it helps to be part of a community. You can always do a retreat on your own, of course, but bringing in other writers, even if it's only by email, will provide inspiration, advice, and a little tough love if you need it. Having this support—and accountability—will ensure that you actually write; the group dynamic helps immeasurably. A few caveats: If you're retreating virtually, stay off the social networks, except perhaps for certain allowable times of day; if you're retreating in person, same goes for the wine.

Clear the decks.

On the first day of my first virtual retreat weekend, I decided that before I began writing I would just do "one little update" to my website, and, as you can imagine, one thing led to another, and six hours passed with no writing getting done. By then I had a headache, so I went for a walk, which ended up being a three-mile hike (albeit lovely—and I saw my first wild turkey ever, so it was worth it). But basically I lost my entire first day because I thought I could take care of one little thing before getting started. Make sure you've taken care of all that you need to do *before* retreating, so you aren't tempted to do anything else that could end up overtaking your writing time.

Create your space.

If you're retreating somewhere else, bring with you whatever you need: notebooks, laptop, books, music, etc. If you're doing a retreat on your own, you may have a place in mind—a quiet café, a library—

or you may be writing at home. If other household members will be there, you'll need to let them know that you're On Retreat and can't be disturbed. Make whatever arrangements you need, from child/pet care to hanging a Do Not Disturb sign on your door. This is your time.

Stay offline.

I don't check email, Twitter, Facebook, or anything else when I'm on a writing retreat, and it's actually quite freeing. It helps when you can retreat on a holiday weekend or some other time during which not much is happening; try to plan your retreat at a time when you won't feel compelled to stay connected. And do whatever you must—from disabling Wi-Fi to going to a café with no Internet access—to be sure you don't interrupt yourself with the lure of the web.

Give yourself guidelines.

Whether it's a timeline (writing from 9 a.m. Friday to 5 p.m. Sunday, for example) or project-related (finishing that first draft of your novel), give yourself clear parameters and stick with them. Figure out what works best for you (you may prefer a time-based schedule to avoid feeling pressured to finish a specific project; on the other hand, if you tend to procrastinate, setting a project-specific goal may be better). If you're retreating with others, be sure you set a schedule of writing time, break times, meals, etc., so that you're not interrupting one another. Then go.

Afterward, assess the pros and cons, the highs and lows.

This will allow you to better plan your next retreat. Did you discover that you were too aimless retreating alone, or too distracted by retreating with others? Do you need to fit more reading time into a retreat weekend? Do you need to stay off the computer and write by hand? Figure out what can make your next retreat more productive and fun, and work it into the plan.

Schedule retreats as often as you can.

Maybe your writing buddies can only get together once a year, but there's no reason you can't do your own retreats eleven other times a year, or more. Plan ahead; make it happen. You need and deserve this time.

Part 2:
Writing exercises

This section offers more than 150 writing prompts to fit any schedule, from five-minute prompts to retreat-length writing exercises. Choose whatever prompt(s) you have time for—and feel free to use them as they are or to rework them in whatever way best fits your mood or project. The only rule here is to put pen to paper, or fingertip to keyboard, and see where it takes you.

Five-minute prompts

Because most of us are writing around our day jobs, families, housework, yard work, pets, and everything else, these prompts are designed to be done in five minutes or fewer and are perfect for the busy writer. (The only bad news about them is that now you have no excuse for not writing.)

Write about what you're wearing on your feet (if anything). Use as many details as time allows.

Describe your last bad haircut.

Write about a time you were late.

~

Describe what you looked like at the age of five.

~

Write about getting caught in the rain.

~

Write about burning dinner.

~

Describe your neighbor's dog.

~

Write about a really bad first date.

Describe the way your house looked on moving day.

Write for one minute about each of these words: cat, sky, lamp, tea, bone.

Write about coffee.

Describe your best friend as a two-year-old.

Write about a new coat.

Describe a bad family photo.

Write about the shape of the clouds.

Write about cocktails at lunch.

Write about waking up before dawn.

Describe the eyes of a loved one.

Write for one minute about each of these words: pomegranate, leaf, pen, orange, fur.

⌒

List what is on the floor of your car or closet.

⌒

Write about a typo.

⌒

Write about a poem you've always remembered.

⌒

Describe how you might look with a different hair color.

⌒

Write about forgetting something at the store.

Describe the air where you are right now.

List your five favorite foods and why.

Write for one minute about each of these words: stage, hill, ear, tomb, glass.

Write about the colors you're wearing.

Describe your most annoying Facebook friend.

⁓

Write about a family pet.

⁓

Write for one minute about each of these words: typewriter, banana, candle, wine, collar.

⁓

Describe your favorite dessert.

⁓

Write about a day at the beach.

⁓

Describe an awkward conversation you had recently.

~

Write about a curtain (and what's behind it).

~

Describe your favorite plant.

~

Write about something you bought or sold.

~

Describe your dream house.

~

Write about snail mail.

~

Write for one minute about each of these words: book, electricity, island, cufflink, blue.

~

Write about your neighbor's cat.

~

Describe where you sit at the family table.

~

Write about an email you wish you hadn't sent.

~

Describe a tree on your street.

~

Write about snow.

~

Describe a language you wish you spoke.

~

Write about stained glass.

~

Describe your childhood bedroom.

~

Write about a nosy neighbor.

~

Write for one minute about each of these words: clock, sand, ballet, kitchen, mitten.

Describe a ritual you have.

Write about bad weather.

Describe a book you'd like to have written.

Five-minute situational prompts

These exercises are more observational in nature—but they're designed to get you writing in the end. These prompts are meant to be habit-forming, in a good way: You should soon be finding inspiration in even the most mundane of places and tasks.

Look at each exercise as a two-step process: Follow the observational guidelines, then make sure you take a few minutes later to jot down what you've witnessed.

In the grocery store line...

Observe those in line around you. Take note of their clothing, hair, faces, expressions. Choose one person in particular who interests you and make mental notes of every detail. As soon as you can, write down all that you remember.

◌

Peer into someone else's grocery cart. Itemize what they're buying, and imagine what they'll do with these items—feed their families, host a party, cook a solitary meal. Envision and write a scene in this person's life.

Watch the entrance and exit doors for a few moments. Observe the way people walk in and how they move: their body language, expressions, clothing, body art, jewelry. Choose a person who interests you and begin a character sketch based on this person.

Waiting for the coffee to brew...

Notice the scents in the air—only the scents, nothing else.

Then, notice the sounds: the gurgle of the coffee pot, any noises coming from outside, etc.

☉

Close your eyes and try to name all the colors that exist in your kitchen.

~

In line at the bank...

Observe the person in line in front of you. Write a description of this person and give him or her a fictional financial history, whether you envision someone who's responsible, cheap, careless, etc.

☉

Imagine that you're in the bank to deposit an unbelievable amount of money—more than you've ever envisioned having. What will you ultimately spend it on?

Think about what you're there at the bank to do—make a deposit, withdraw money. What are you grateful for in this moment?

⌒

Waiting for the kids to get out of school...

Look around you and choose two random strangers, whether they're teachers, crossing guards, or passersby. Then have the two of them meet: What do they talk about?

Observe what kids are wearing. Then think about what you wore when you were their age(s). Write about the similarities and differences.

Write about the one thing you feel is most important to teach the children in your life.

~

In line at the post office...

Imagine the route your envelope, package, etc., will take to get to its destination. What would it see along the way?

○

Write about the last love letter you wrote, and the last one you received.

○

Look at the person in front of you in line, then the person behind you. Imagine these two as a couple: Might they be compatible, or not? And why?

Fifteen-minute prompts

These prompts are for when you have more than a few minutes at hand but less time than a prolonged writing session offers. Feel free to go for less or even more than fifteen minutes; write for as long as time allows.

~

Pull a random item out of your purse or wallet or backpack and write a full page about it: what it looks like, feels like; how old it is; where it came from, etc.

~

Choose a favorite piece of music. Listen to it and write about the first time you heard it. Include as many details as possible: where you were, what you wore, what time of year it was, what time of day. Aim to write at least two pages ... and let the piece wander wherever it wants to go.

~

The senses:

Write about the scent of happiness.

Write about the texture of anxiety.

Write about the sound of despair.

~

Write about a time you guessed wrong about something, whether it was who might be calling, whom your daughter would marry, or how the polenta would turn out.

~

Write about something you lost. Next, write about something you found.

Consider physical objects lost or found—a watch, an

earring, a wallet—but feel free to go beyond to such things as the loss of a job or innocence, the finding of your calling or true love.

~

Write a bad sentence. Make it sloppy in every way you can, from style to punctuation. Then note which bad habits came naturally and which you had to work at. Revise a work in progress, paying special attention to your weak spots.

~

Close calls in life give us a sense of who we are, whether it's a near accident or a more emotional close call, such as awaiting a test result. And if you write fiction, writing about a character's close call offers a telling glimpse into his/her heart and mind as well as shows us how he or she might act in a given situation. Write about a close call.

~

Sometimes the simplest writing exercise can yield the most interesting material—and this is one of my favorites; I turn to it whenever I'm stuck, and it never fails to go somewhere unexpected. Choose an object in the room; better yet, take a quick walk around and choose several. Then spend fifteen minutes writing about each one, letting the object tell its own story.

Being random can be the best solution for a tricky revision or when you're simply looking for inspiration. Go to a bookshelf, run your fingers along the spines, and pick a book. Open it to a random page. Run your fingers along the page, stopping three times; each time, write down the words you land on. (If it's a word such as "the" or "and," use the previous word instead.) Write for five minutes about each of these random words, and see what sort of magic happens.

Write about one of the "Hallmark holidays" you despise, from Mother's Day to Valentine's Day. Then write about one you love (perhaps it's the same holiday). Finally, write about a holiday you'd create if you could make up a new one for all the world to celebrate.

~

Write about a costume, personality, job, etc., that you (or your main character) has always wanted to try on. Maybe you're not musical but have always longed to sing; perhaps you're a blonde who's always wanted to be a redhead; maybe you dream of being a pastry chef. Write about a day of living this other life—and see where it takes you.

~

Write about a lie someone told you. Include everything, from how and when you knew it was a lie to what might have been different if you'd been told the truth.

~

Write about a favorite painting. Go into great detail

visually; also include background on the artist, including when and where the painting was created, if you can.

~

Write about a rejection, whether it's an unrequited love or a poem returned with a form letter. Write about the way it makes you feel—physically, emotionally—and the first thing you did right after being rejected.

~

Open your fridge; write about what's inside. Make a list of items and use this to explore how you feel about these items: why they're there, what they say about you, what you'd like to be different, and anything else you can think of.

~

Remember a time when a decision was essentially made for you (where you'd be living, due to a parent's or a partner's new job; a transfer at your own job; an assignment you didn't want; a

medical decision you felt you had to make; etc.).
Write about how it affected you, how you might
have chosen differently, and why.

Late at night, a dog barks outside. Write about what
you think it sees: a rabbit, a stranger, another dog,
its owner. Where does your imagination first take
you—and why?

Fifteen-minute situational prompts

These exercises are for those slightly longer moments in which you're waiting for something or someone (at the dentist's office, for example), as well as for the quieter moments of an otherwise engaging activity (like waiting for your child's turn at a music recital). Pull out your notebook and write in the moment, if possible, or simply observe, making notes in your head to be written down later.

And feel free to adapt these exercises to best fit your own life in whatever ways you wish—for example, if you're a full-time parent, change "staff meeting" to something else: a PTA meeting, a book club gathering, etc.; if you're a freelancer, change this to a client meeting or a conference session.

In the doctor's waiting room...

Look at the magazines on the tables. Which ones are you most drawn to—and why? And which magazines do you feel you *should* read as opposed to the ones you really *want* to read?

○

Choose one person in the room—a fellow patient,
a waiting child, a receptionist—and observe the
physical characteristics of this person. When you
can, write down everything to the very last detail.
Then create a fictional character based on this
description.

○

Take a moment to assess your mood. Are you
anxious, bored, depressed, happy, curious? Align
your emotions with the following: the reason for
your visit; your childhood perception of doctors,
health, illness, and wellness; and how you feel about
your doctor.

While you're making dinner...

Observe each ingredient as it makes its way into the
dish you're preparing. How did each one get chosen:
at random, a family recipe, a new recipe? Write about

the history of the meal you're preparing, from when you first made it to how it's been received when prepared for others.

◯

Think about the process of cooking: Do you enjoy it? Is it a chore or a pleasure? Are you the household cook, do you take turns with others, or is cooking a rarity for you? When did you cook your very first meal on your own—as a child, in college, for a date, as a newlywed, etc.? What is it specifically that you like (or dislike) about cooking?

◯

Sneak a bite of something as you're preparing the meal. Take a moment to focus on the tastes and textures of this bite. Where do your thoughts turn when you taste this particular item? Does it remind you of any place, situation, or person? If so, what, when, who?

At a child's music recital...

As you watch the young musicians on stage, think about your own relationship to music. What instruments do/did you play? Did you embrace it, or were lessons forced upon you? How do you feel about those instruments today? What place does music have in your life now, and how closely does this reflect how you grew up?

☾

As you watch the child you're there to see—whether it's your own child, a niece or nephew, grandchild, etc.—imagine that child ten years from now, then twenty. How do you envision this child's life evolving? Will the instrument he/she is playing now still be a part of his/her life?

☾

Choose one random person in the room. Imagine life if you had met this person instead of your current partner. In what ways would your life be the same, and in what ways might it be different? What would your family think of this person? In what ways do you imagine you'd be compatible, or not?

⁓

In the security line at the airport...

Take a moment to remember what flying was like when you were a small child. Did you have a fear of flying or a fearlessness about it? How is that the same or different from the way you feel about flying today?

◡

Try to remember the last stranger you spoke with on a flight. Write down as much of the conversation as you can remember. When you run out of memory, begin to re-create the dialogue, continuing until you have an entire scene—and a new character as well.

◡

What book(s) are you taking with you on your

travels, and why? Write about what you like to read, listen to, and/or watch while traveling. Write about the difference between traveling for pleasure (for a vacation) versus traveling for other reasons (business, family issues, etc.).

Study the person in front of you. Where do you think he or she is going—and what visual, verbal, or gestural clues give you that impression?

During a staff meeting....

Look around at your colleagues and note their expressions. Remember, or jot down, what you see on their faces—the features only, such as turned-down lips or furrowed brows. Then note what you read from their expressions: Do they seem engaged, bored, interested, elsewhere? How does this compare to your own mood, and what does this tell you about your colleagues and your work?

Think back: to your major in college, to your favorite class in high school, to what you wanted to be when you grew up. How closely does your current career align with what you always wanted to do? In what ways have you followed your passions, and in what ways would you like to follow them even more?

Write about sustenance. This can take any number of forms here: what you and/or your colleagues are drinking/eating during your meeting; what parts of the job fulfill you the most; or what you need to do for yourself in order to perform well at work. Try writing this from the third person perspective (the *he/she* voice).

During a holiday dinner...

Observe the foods on the table. How are these

similar to and different from the foods you grew up with, from how they were prepared to how they are presented?

Choose two people at the table and imagine they are something they aren't: If they're siblings, imagine them as mother/daughter or father/son; if they're grandparent/grandchild, reverse the relationship. Write a scene featuring these two characters in this new and different context.

Consider where you want to be during this holiday meal. Are you exactly where you'd like to be—and if so, why? And if not, where might you prefer to be, and why?

While in a phone conversation with in-laws...

Note the tones and nuances of the voice of the person you're talking with. Think about how this voice is similar to and different from that of your partner. What characteristics seem to have been passed down, and which ones have not?

○

Imagine you grew up with your partner's family rather than your own, and vice versa. How might the two of you have turned out differently or the same? Would you still have ended up together? How might you have handled your partner's unique set of challenges had you grown up in his/her family instead?

○

Write about a day in the life of your partner as a small child. Imagine any parts of his/her life that you may not know, and feel free to invent anything you wish. You can write this from the POV of your partner, his or her parents, a sibling, etc.

While in the dentist's chair...

Most people have very definite feelings about visiting the dentist: It's either a nightmarish experience or a perfectly pleasant one. What are your feelings about going to the dentist? Do you dread it—and if so, why? Or has it always been a pleasant experience— and if so, why? Reach back for the reasons behind your experience, and go beyond the dentist to other such visits: doctor, therapist, etc.

○

Think about your smile. Do you use it often or seldom? How often do you fake it? What are the things that genuinely bring a smile to your face— and under what circumstances do you find yourself forcing a smile you're not feeling?

○

Write about a visit to the dentist/orthodontist that

changed your teeth in some way. This could be the first time you had a tooth pulled or the day you walked out with new braces (or the day the braces came off). Was the procedure one that was noticeable to the world (braces), or not (cavity, pulled tooth)? Write about how you felt about the public/personal change for the rest of that day.

~

At the hair salon/barber shop...

Think about the last time you made a major change to your hair, whether it was a drastic haircut or a new color. What inspired you to make the change? Did your new appearance make you feel any different?

◯

Hair stylists are known for being great talkers and/ or great listeners. Write about something you've told your stylist that few other people know—then write about something your stylist told you that surprised you.

Imagine you could have a complete makeover, anything from a new haircut to plastic surgery. What would you change about your appearance, or would you leave it exactly the same? Why/why not? And how do you envision it might change your life?

During halftime at a sporting event ...

Whether you're at your child's soccer game or the World Series, look around you and observe the crowd. Take a few mental notes (or real ones, if you can), and write a character based on the one who strikes you as the most interesting. If you can, find an entire family to observe for a few moments, and write a scene based around a dinner at home with this family.

Consider your relationship to sports. Are you (or

were you once) an athlete? How has this part of your life changed or evolved over the years? Do you prefer team sports or individual feats of athleticism? Write about your history, from childhood to present, of sports and physical fitness, including details from your family members' athletic history as well.

◯

If you could choose one sport to excel at—i.e., at a professional level—what would it be and why? Or, if you are a professional athlete already, what sport might you choose if you could do it all over again with a different one?

Evening writing prompts

These prompts are designed for a time when you have an entire evening of writing at hand (or a morning or afternoon, for that matter). Allow yourself to get immersed in these exercises and to explore where they take you, whether as a personal exercise or as something that informs your current project.

Whether it's for a weekend getaway, a two-week vacation, or a move to another state, when you're packing your bags, you have to consider what to take and what to leave behind—in other words, what's important and why. Think about this in the context of your life, or your character's. How much of what we need is already with us, and how much of it exists in the things we own? Begin here: If you could pack up only one suitcase to last you the rest of your life, what would be in it?

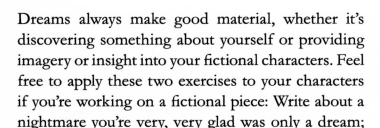

Dreams always make good material, whether it's discovering something about yourself or providing imagery or insight into your fictional characters. Feel free to apply these two exercises to your characters if you're working on a fictional piece: Write about a nightmare you're very, very glad was only a dream; and write about a dream you wish could be reality.

Write about a job you were really bad at—or, if you're writing fiction, write about this in the context of one of your characters. Go into as much detail as possible: the first day on the job, a typical awful day, the day you/he/she gets fired, etc.

You've probably had the sensation of waking up in a hotel or at someone else's house and being momentarily disoriented because you think you're home, and it takes you a few moments to realize where you are. The feeling is a little strange and frightening—but also interesting and invigorating, as anything unfamiliar can be. Let this exercise take you to places, situations, and feelings unknown and unexplored: Write about waking up in a strange place.

~

Take out a work in progress—a story, poem, novel, anything at all. The only requirement is that it is unfinished. (Better yet, choose something you're really stuck on.) After reading it over, write a glowing review of it, as if you're a book or magazine reviewer. The idea is to sing the praises of this piece as you'd like it to be when it's finished. Finally, compare your review to the work as it is now and see if writing the review has helped you identify or overcome any issues you can now revise.

~

This one is simple but can take you far; don't hold back. Write about a mistake you made. Include all the details you can, and try to create an entire scene, complete with setting, dialogue, and backstory.

＊

When I'm creating new characters, I try to know all I can about them—and knowing their regrets is always a big help; regrets turn out to be a big part of who they are. So, whether you're exploring your own stories or those of fictional characters, write about regret. Let this exercise take you far and wide.

＊

Many of us have a collection of things that were gathered during our infancy: birth announcements, baby shoes, etc. Take out your own box of baby stuff, if you have one. If you don't, imagine it: What's inside? What parts of your life might be contained there that you can't possibly remember? Whether you're writing from your own POV or that of one of your characters, take this exercise as far as you can, from the just-born person to the person of today.

＊

This prompt evokes the adage "write what you know," only it'll take you a little further. First, choose something in which you're an expert, whether it's playing the piano or dentistry or gardening. Write two pages about this (it can be a personal story, a poem, or a scene in a fictional piece). Next, choose something similar but about which you know a lot less, or nothing at all (for example, if you're an expert at the piano, write about the oboe; if you're a dentist, write about being an obstetrician, etc.). Write two pages, following the guidelines above.

Write about a detour, large or small. Try this one in two different ways: first in verse, as a poem, then in prose, as a fully developed scene.

Go online and search for images of a place you've always wanted to visit. View everything from strangers' vacation photos to historical images to professional and encyclopedic photographs. Study them for a few minutes, then log out. Next, write a scene, poem, or story set in this place, from what you recall of the images as well as how you imagine it to be.

Often what gets neglected in a scene—at least, in my first drafts it does—is a sense of where the characters are physically. Yet these details can tell us so much about the characters' personalities, their relationships to others in the scene, and how they feel about what is happening. So take a scene you're working on and think like a stage director. Note where each character is, whether he or she is standing, sitting, pacing. Get these characters in their places—wherever they need to be to reveal what's happening in the scene, how they feel about it, and where they're headed from here.

There are certain things that annoy us—leaf blowers at seven o'clock on a Saturday morning, for example, or typos on billboards—and, naturally, what annoys us can also reveal quite a lot about us, just as our characters' pet peeves reveal a lot about them. Write about your (or your main character's) top three pet peeves. Then write about why and how they came about, i.e., what might be the origin of these particular peeves?

Imagine you're taking a walk at night, and you see into your neighbors' lighted kitchen, witnessing some sort of confrontation. Write about the argument, making it as fictional as you need to. Come back to this prompt, switching to another neighbor or another neighborhood entirely.

Think of a pet (one you have now or a childhood pet) and write about a day in its life. Cover the whole day: everything you think your pet does and thinks about, who else it may see during the day, and anything else you can think of.

Evening situational prompts

These prompts are meant to take the moment at hand and stretch beyond it, whether personally or through the eyes of your character(s). As always, feel free to rework these prompts however you'd like—to replace "night" with "day," for example.

⁓

Write about what it means to have a night off. Where would you go, and why would you choose to spend the evening in this particular place?

⁓

What would your main character do with a night off? What would his/her primary love interest do? Would they be together or apart?

If you could do anything you wanted tonight—from robbing a bank to having an affair—with absolutely no consequences, what would you do? Describe the evening in great detail.

Envision the following: A couple is at home one evening, and the power goes out. To add a little drama, make it a sub-zero winter evening or a sweltering summer night. Write about how this event might drive the couple apart or bring them closer together. (Try this one again with an older couple, or a younger one—or two estranged siblings.)

When was your last girls'/guys' night out? Write a scene entirely in dialogue—imagine the scene as part of a play or a film—that reveals one of the conversations from that night out. Feel free to let the dialogue cross over into fiction at any time.

~

Write about a time you met someone new on an evening out, whether at a college bar or a PTA meeting. Describe this person in detail. Next, write about meeting this person in an entirely different context (if you met in a bar, change this to a doctor's office; if you met in a class, change this to a casino). Let the characters evolve, and see where the exercise takes you.

~

Write about the last time you did something outside your comfort zone, from going to the movies alone to cooking Thanksgiving dinner for your extended family. What were your fears or reservations? How did it feel to do this before, during, and afterward?

Vacation-day writing prompts

These exercises are for extended writing sessions, designed to allow you to delve more deeply into your work.

~

Have you ever had one of those moments in which you wonder whether something might have turned out differently in your life? If you'd taken one job over another, if you'd missed the elevator on which you met the love of your life, if you'd reached the intersection two seconds later. We can look back on these moments and feel either fortunate or unlucky. Explore this idea in these two prompts: Write about a moment you wished had turned out differently, and write about a moment you're grateful for.

~

This three-part exercise is all about confinement, about getting stuck, whether it's imposed on us or by our own doing. Fiction writers: If you don't feel like writing about yourself, apply these exercises to your characters.

- Write about a time you had to do something you didn't want to do—whether it was something that was "for your own good," like finishing your peas, or something necessary but unpleasant, like a flu shot or taking your wild, beastly cat to the vet.

- Write about a time you were physically confined (stuck in an airport, trapped in a stalled subway car, imprisoned in a jail cell). Include all the details you can, including a little backstory for context.

- Write about a time you felt emotionally trapped (in a relationship, a job, etc.). Again, include all the details and backstory you can.

Rumors provide fantastic material for writers—the weirder and more outlandish they are, the better. As writers, we don't care whether the rumor about a long-lost classmate's love child is actually true; we're just fascinated by the possibility that it might be because there's a story there. Whether a rumor is about a tornado warning, a sneaky colleague, or a relative having an affair, hearing such things perks us up, makes us pay attention. It teaches us to be alert, a state we should always be in as writers. Keep this in mind even after you try this prompt: Write about a rumor you heard. Try to write out several scenes, using these details: who started it, who is spreading it, whom the rumor is about.Write around the rumor itself, exploring instead the reasons it came into being.

Write about a decision that you or your character needs to make. Write about making this decision, in two versions: one in which you weigh the pros and cons and make a thoughtful, informed decision; then write another in which you just go for it. Don't forget to write about the consequences for each scenario.

This two-part prompt allows you to see your character from another POV—and it's also fun because it often leads to great conflicts. The first one is for fiction writers, the second for nonfiction/memoir writers—but I hope you'll try them both.

- Write about two characters gossiping about your protagonist.

- Write about a time you overheard someone talking about you without knowing you could hear.

Traveling, even if not very far from home, opens our minds to new possibilities—and especially to new characters. When you try this two-part prompt, let it take you wherever it wants to go.

- Think of someone you saw while traveling. Write a description of this person.

- Next, write a description of yourself from this person's POV.

As a writer, you need to create tension in your stories, which means creating conflict. And this means showing us the not-so-honorable sides of human beings. This doesn't mean your characters have to be terrible people—it means only that they need to show us their secret dark sides. And they need to surprise us. So write about your character's—or your own—dark side. This can be a secret wish, a family secret, a forbidden relationship—anything that might cause your character (or you) either to act out or to hide.

Most scenes should offer a sense of place, yet often setting doesn't emerge until we've solved other issues first. This prompt is more of a revision exercise, designed to infuse your work with a stronger sense of setting.

Take a scene from your writing project that lacks a sense of the physical. Add details, including where the scene takes place; how it looks, feels, smells, sounds; what the lighting conditions are; and what the weather is. Make sure that the setting you create reflects the mood and tone of the scene itself.

⁓

Stretching the mind, preferably into uncomfortable territory, is often where the best and most surprising things can happen in your work. So, for example, if you're not scientific, find a periodic table of elements. Pick a metal (gold, bronze, zinc, lithium, silver, tin) or a gas (helium, krypton), and write about it for ten minutes. Likewise, if you're not musical, pick an instrument you've always wanted to play (piano, oboe, accordion, tuba), and write about it for ten minutes. If you don't know the right words and terms, make them up. Write with authority. Have fun with it. Then, work what you've written into a scene, either from your own life or your main character's.

⁓

Write about a time when something small—a chocolate bar, a smile from the right person at the right time, a martini—made you happy. Then write about a time when you felt happy about your life as a whole. Write a scene, whether imagined or real, that combines the two. Finally, write a scene that takes place the day before—and another that takes place the day after.

~

Write about a time when you (or your main character) felt angry. This could be over something small, such as someone cutting in line at the local café, or something bigger, such as your partner not listening at a time when you need it. Write out the scene as it happened, i.e., in which you reacted as you normally do, either by expressing or holding back your anger. Next, write out the scene in the opposite way, in which you did the reverse of what comes naturally.

Vacation-day situational prompts

These exercises can be applied to your characters as well as your own life; write for as long as you can and see what evolves.

⌒

Think about the last time you were in an airport, whether it was for business or pleasure. Where were you going, and with whom? Write about the trip and how you felt about it (eager? apprehensive?). Next, write a scene in which your flight gets detoured to another destination entirely. Where do you end up, and what do you do once you arrive?

⌒

Give yourself (or your main character) a day off. What would you do with your day? Where would you go, who would you see—and why? Include as much detail as you can, revealing hour by hour how you (or your character) would spend this day.

Describe your last sick day (or the last time you faked a sick day). What did you have (or pretend to have)? Write about what being sick is like for you, beginning with how illness was treated in your family as you grew up—were you pampered or left alone, rewarded or punished for being ill? Next, write about how you treat yourself when you're not feeling well.

Write about a staycation. What would you do if you had an entire day, or a week, to spend in your hometown as if you were a tourist? What would you see and do? What sights and activities have you not done yet in your own city?

Write about how you'd spend a day if you were in Paris. In Nairobi. In Buenos Aires. (Feel free to add more and more destinations; you can also apply this exercise to any of your characters.)

~

This is a prompt you can do over and over again: Find a map or a globe, close your eyes, and let your hand wander over it. Stop and note where your index finger is. Wherever you landed, write about what your life might've been like had you grown up in this place instead of your own hometown. Next, write about traveling to your hometown as a tourist from this other place.

Weekend writing prompts

These writing exercises will help you jump-start a weekend of writing—or whenever it is you're able to spend a couple of days immersed in your creative work.

~

To every action there is an equal and opposite reaction—for the laws of motion as well as for characters. Without getting into physics here, let's look at this in terms of character, i.e., the idea that from a writerly perspective, this means conflict— and this is where the fun begins. Take two characters and put them into a situation in which they do not agree (this can be anything from where to have dinner to whether or not to have children). Then write. You can write this as dialogue, from one character's POV or from both—the only condition is that neither character gives in.

~

With each new season, everything shifts: We get out our happy lamps or our flip-flops; we plan our vacations or head back to school. Each season has significance, though we don't often stop to ponder it. For this prompt, spend some time writing about each season—what you feel about it, how much you love/hate it, how it temporarily alters your life. (Fiction writers: Feel free to apply this one to any of your characters.) Begin with spring, move on to summer and autumn, and end with winter.

~

When writing fiction, the fun part is creating characters who can behave badly (at least, I find this a lot of fun). In real life, most of us are all-too-aware of the consequences of what we say and do; we're generally careful and law-abiding. But sometimes, wouldn't it be a lot more interesting not to be? Write about a character who does something without thinking of the consequences. (Or, for all you memoirists out there, write about a time you did this.) It needn't be too outrageous, but it should be something this character wouldn't normally do, whether it's playing hooky from work or stealing something from a friend. Include the moment he/she makes the decision to go forward as well as the consequences of his/her actions.

~

There is never too much you can know about your characters (whether in fiction or memoir)—and while there is a limit to what you can fit on the page, don't let this stop you from exploring all angles as part of your writing process. Here are a few character-related prompts (feel free to apply them to yourself or a real-life character if you're writing memoir or personal essay):

- Write about your character's favorite piece of jewelry (it could be something he/she owns, or something he/she covets).

- Write about your character's biggest disappointment.

- Write about your character's secret wish—the one he/she hasn't shared with anyone, ever.

For this exercise, you'll write two scenes, and they can either be personal or fictional.

First, write a scene about a death. It can be witnessing a death, learning about a death, or any other way you choose to portray the scene—however you choose to write it, be as detailed as possible; include dialogue, a sense of place, etc. Next, write about a birth. Again, be as detailed as possible. Finally, take a look at the language in each of these scenes. What are the similarities, the differences? What words and images attract and/or repel? What connections can you find, if any?

Think of someone you knew for only a short time—a classmate, a colleague, someone you dated or played a sport with—anyone who appeared in, then disappeared from, your life. Write down everything you remember about this person. Using these memories, write about what he/she brought to your life during that brief period. Next, create a fictional character based on this person.

Weekend situational prompts

Write about a first weekend away in a new relationship (this can be either a personal story or a scene with one of your characters). What went well, and what went wrong? What did each person learn about the other? Include as much detail as possible, from what they wore to what they talked about.

~

Write about what your ideal summer day would look like. What would you do; where would you go; with whom would you spend this day? Then, write about the perfect autumn day. Then, the perfect winter day and, finally, the perfect spring day.

~

Write about money. If you're well-off, imagine losing

what you have and how this might change your life. Would it be devastating or freeing? Where and how would you now live? How would your life change for better or for worse? And, if you're not well-off, imagine that you've just come into a lot of money. What would you do with it, and why? Next, write about the source of the money: How might your enjoyment of it and your ways of spending it be different if you'd earned it yourself versus if you'd inherited it or won it in a lottery?

Choose a favorite painting by a famous portrait artist and study it for a while: its color, textures, lighting, subject. Next, imagine yourself as the subject of one of this artist's paintings. How do you feel being observed? How might this artist capture your character and personality on the canvas? Do you imagine he/she would see you differently than you see yourself? Let your imagination roam for this exercise, and feel free to apply it to your character(s) as well.

Imagine your life if one thing about yourself, major or minor, were different. Create a list of possibilities, then choose one (you can always return to this exercise later and choose another). For example: being born a girl instead of a boy, or vice versa; being born in a different part of the country or the world; being born to different parents; being educated elsewhere or differently; choosing another career or partner; having more children or none; being blonde instead of brunette; being tall instead of short...and on and on.

~

Envision being away for a dream retreat in a very remote location, like an island or a cabin in the woods. Then imagine that you must trade your normal location for this "dreamlike" spot. How would you adapt to living in your supposedly ideal world, cut off from most of the everyday things you're accustomed to?

Retreat writing prompts

These multi-step prompts are ideal for when you've got several days or weeks to devote to your writing or when you're ready to generate new material.

⁓

Stories begin from curiosity—and often this stems from someone we see who seems mysterious (he or she may not be, but it's what we don't know that always intrigues us the most). So, in the spirit of creating mystery, choose someone you see semi-regularly (your barista, the checkout clerk at the supermarket, the jogger you pass on the trail, etc.), and write at least two pages about this person as you see him or her every day.

- Next, write down what you imagine this person was doing the day before you saw him/her.

- Then, write about what you imagine he or she will be doing the day after.

- Finally, write a scene in which you connect with this person, in an entirely different context. (Feel free to use one of your fictional characters instead.) How does he/she look in this different context? What do you talk about?

Pick an old photo out of a box or an album (yes, this means a photo so old it's from the pre–digital camera days). (Note: If you are so young as not to remember pre–digital camera days, simply pick the oldest photo you can find on your smartphone or laptop or iPad or whatever. And rejoice in your youth.) Next, write about three things:

- Write about what you were doing the day/night the photo was taken.

- Write about that time in your life and where you thought you were headed next.

- Write about where you are now and how

you feel about looking back on that time (nostalgic, sad, happy, etc.).

⁓

The following exercise is designed to jump-start a story or novel (or, if you're writing memoir, to mine the past for material for a scene; simply use real characters, conversations, and details). This prompt can be done in any number of ways, depending on how you prefer to write. You can set a timer and work in ten-minute intervals, then go back, see what you've got, and flesh out the story. Or you can go a little deeper and write in twenty- or thirty-minute intervals. Or you can simply give yourself as much time as you need for each section.

1. Imagine a character.

- Describe the character via his/her driver's license (physical appearance, driving history, whether he/she is an organ donor, etc.).

- Describe his/her profession (include educational background, work history, physical location of the job).

- Write about his/her family (identify the most important person in this character's life; describe his/her nemesis; write about his/her current and childhood homes).

2. Write a scene.

- Put your character in conversation with his/her nemesis (begin using only dialogue).

- Next, describe where they are as they have this conversation (include how they met up, what season it is, what time of day, all the details you can).

- Provide some interior monologue (what does your character want? what is he/she getting or not getting from this conversation?).

3. Go deeper into the story.

- Write a scene that immediately follows the one you've just written (i.e., what does your character do next?).

- Describe something that has changed, for one or both characters, after the meeting they had. What are their states of mind now as opposed to before?

- Write about the next time these two meet. Where is it? How long has it been—hours, weeks, years, decades? How does each character look and feel? How do they treat each other? Is there any sense of resolution here, or has either of them gained insight into his/her own life based on the nature of the relationship?

⁓

In this two-part exercise, first you'll create a scrapbook or collage, in any size, shape, or form you wish. Include images, poetry, prose, anything and everything that inspires you—but do use a mix of words and images. Most important, don't think as you put it together—just let your hands move and place the various pieces wherever they want to go.

Next, do the following prompts based on the scrapbook or collage you've created.

- Choose one image and write for five minutes.

- Choose two images and combine them to create a scene.

- Choose an image and a word-based section (a poem, a sentence, etc.) and write a poem or scene that contains both.

- Look at the images and words you've selected. Pick a word that sums up the various parts of your collage/scrapbook. Write about this word.

- Write a scene about a stranger discovering your collage/scrapbook and what he or she will infer about you. Then write about a close family member finding it.

When I begin a new piece of writing, it's usually after many ideas have come together and simmered for a while in my brain—only then do I get a sense of the possibilities. This exercise offers a way to combine seemingly random information, mix it up a bit, and see what comes together. The prompt is designed so that you can return to it again and again; have some notepaper or index cards handy for shuffling.

- Write a list of something (it can be anything at all—for example: your favorite foods or books, your closest friends, the places you want to travel to, the errands you need to do today, etc.).

- Next, write down your impressions about each of these things as you saw them at the age of five, then the age of ten, then fifteen, and so on. (What were your favorite foods then; who were your best friends; where did you want to visit; what did dry cleaning or grocery shopping mean to you, if anything?)

- Next, choose two impressions (for example, your best friend at five years old and your best friend at twenty) and combine these two things in a scene. This will take some creative license—you may have two people, or you may have two inanimate objects. Add the people, setting, details, and anything else you need to create a scene.

- Choose another combination of impressions and write another scene.

- Finally, read over and compare the two scenes. How are they alike and different? What stands out to you as something you'd like to explore further? Have any characters and/or settings emerged that can play a role in a current or future project?

～

For this exercise, you can write from personal experience or through the eyes of one of your fictional characters.

- Write a scene about a former partner: the first time you met. Was it love/attraction at first sight, or were you actually quite unlikely to have ended up together? Include as many details as you can in this scene, including dialogue and a sense of physical space.

- Next, write a scene about the first night you spent together—it can be a sex scene but doesn't necessarily have to be; the focus here is "first" and all that this entails.

- Write about an unexpected joy, whether it's a small, specific one (like a time he/she surprised you with a gift or gesture) or a more general one (like an overall feeling of peace or contentment).

- Write about a disappointment—either a time you felt disappointed by your partner or a time you disappointed him/her.

- Finally, write about the last time you were together. Did you know then that it would be the last? Did your partner? What are the main differences between this scene and the first?

Write a scene in which you combine the following items, or elements thereof. Apply it to fictional characters if you'd like, and try it multiple times using various aspects of the items on the list.

- your hometown

- your mother's/father's profession

- your best friends in high school

- your favorite books

- your first job

- what you're wearing right now

Retreat situational prompts

Write about being around people: Is this a normal, comfortable, happy state for you? Or, given the choice, do you prefer to be alone? Why or why not? Offer details on how you feel, physically and emotionally, in both situations. Write a scene that offers insight into how you came to be this way. Feel free to apply this exercise to your character(s) as well.

When you're online—whether it's Facebook or email—does your online persona differ from the real, live you? Do you feel as though you're exactly the same, or do you present yourself differently virtually than you do in person? Explore the reasons and interpretations that this insight can offer.

Stay offline for an entire day or, even better, an entire weekend. How does it feel to be "disconnected"? What do you spend your time doing instead? Write about a time in your life when you didn't have the same access to the virtual world that you do now. How has being online changed your life, and what are the positive and negative results of this connectivity in your life?

Write about breaking a habit. Include all the details, from how the habit began to how it escalated to when you realized you had to give it up. Write about how your life is different now that you no longer have this particular habit.

Write about a particular time you were in class, whether a college course, a karate lesson, a cooking class, etc.—choose any class that stands out to you, and note why. What did you learn in this particular class that has stuck with you, and what made it stick? Think about possibilities from the quality of instruction to the relevance of the subject matter to your life.

~

If you could hop into a time machine, would you go forward or back—and why? Write about where you would go, what time period, and what you would hope to experience. Include the people you'd meet and use all the details you can.

~

If you could freeze time and take a retreat any time you needed it (returning at the exact time you left), when would you most often choose to escape? Where would you go, and how long would you stay?

Appendix:
A few good resources

There are dozens and dozens of wonderful writing resources out there—far more than I can list here. Below are a few of my own current and longtime favorites.

When I'm not making up my own writing prompts, I'm constantly turning to Judy Reeves's *A Writer's Book of Days* for prompts and inspiration. Bonni Goldberg's *Room to Write* also offers daily exercises and encouragement. And *Naming the World*, edited by Bret Anthony Johnston, offers prompts as well as craft advice from dozens of writers on everything from character to point of view to dialogue.

Julia Cameron's *The Artist's Way* and *The Vein of Gold* remain classics in the field of creativity and inspiration, as do Natalie Goldberg's many books: Try *Writing Down the Bones, Wild Mind,* and *Old Friend from Far Away: The Practice of Writing Memoir.*

~

Anne Lamott's *Bird by Bird* is still among my favorite books about writing ever.

~

The Writer magazine offers practical advice for writers as well as writing prompts on its website, as does *Poets & Writers.*

~

I'm always inspired by reading about other writers' processes. If you haven't already, visit *The Paris Review* Interviews (www.theparisreview.org/interviews), which features amazing interviews with authors from the 1950s onward.

And you might also enjoy Kristin Bair O'Keefe's "Writerhead Wednesday," in which Kristin writes about the state of *writerhead* (those dreamlike writing moments in which the rest of the world disappears) and interviews authors on what their own experiences of writerhead are like. To check it out, visit www.kristinbairokeeffe.com.

There are literally dozens of blogs offering writing prompts, with more starting all the time, so I'd suggest doing a web search and bookmarking the ones you like (and looking for new ones every couple of months). To give you a place to start: You'll find weekly writing prompts at my blog, **Remembering English** (www.midgeraymond.com/blog), and for those of you who'd like a daily dose, **The Write Prompts** blog (www.thewriteprompts.com) offers prompts seven days a week.

And, finally, for a little of everything, author Erika Dreifus writes an amazingly comprehensive blog, **Practicing Writing** (www.erikadreifus.com/blogs/practicing-writing), where you'll find information on everything from writing prompts to submissions opportunities.

About the author

Midge Raymond has been a writer, editor, and teacher for more than twenty years and has been a creativity coach for more than a decade. She has created writing prompts for classes and workshops in settings from university classrooms to homeless shelters. Midge has taught at Boston University, Grub Street Writers, San Diego Writers, and Richard Hugo House, among others.

Midge's short story collection, *Forgetting English*, received the Spokane Prize for Short Fiction. Originally published by Eastern Washington University Press, the book has been reissued in an expanded edition by Press 53. Her stories have appeared in numerous literary journals and magazines—among them *TriQuarterly, American Literary Review, Bellingham Review, Indiana Review, North American Review, Bellevue Literary Review*, the *Los Angeles Times* magazine, and many others—and have received several Pushcart Prize nominations.

Midge writes about the writing life for such publications as *The Writer* as well as on her blog, **Remembering English** (www.midgeraymond. com/blog), which features a new writing prompt every week. For more information, visit Midge online at www.MidgeRaymond.com.

**Ashland
Creek
Press**

Ashland Creek Press is a small, independent publisher of books with a world view. From travel narratives to eco-literature, our mission is to publish a range of books that foster an appreciation for worlds outside our own, for nature and the animal kingdom, for the creative process, and for the ways in which we all connect. To keep up-to-date on new and forthcoming works, subscribe to our free newsletter by visiting: www.AshlandCreekPress.com.

CPSIA information can be obtained at www.ICGtesting.com
Printed in the USA
LVOW040802260812

295918LV00004B/5/P

9 781618 220110